BATTLES OF THE CIVIL
Antietam

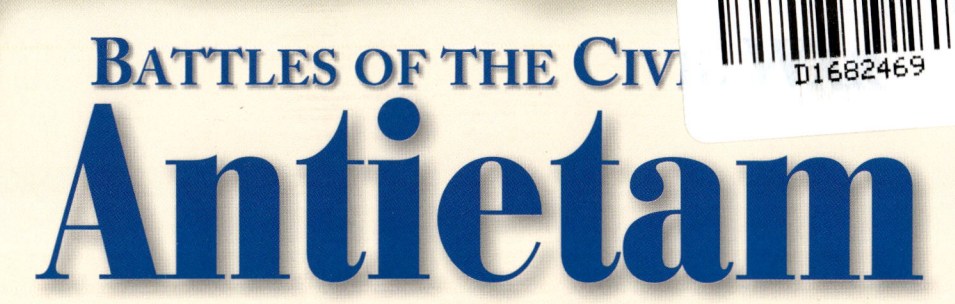

by Daniel Rosen

Table of Contents

Introduction 2
Chapter 1
Background to Battle 6
Chapter 2
The Bloodiest Day in American History 14
Chapter 3
A Different World 24
Conclusion 29
Solve This Answers 30
Glossary 31
Index 32

Introduction

One issue decided the election for president of the United States in 1860. The issue was slavery. Slavery was legal in the South. It was not legal in the North. The South was afraid the government would pass laws ending slavery.

Four men ran for president that year. Abraham Lincoln won. Lincoln said he would not make laws ending slavery in the South. But he said he did not want slavery to spread to the **territories**. These were newly settled areas that were not yet states.

The South did not believe Lincoln. Southern leaders said if Lincoln won the election, they would **secede** (sih-SEED). Their states would leave the United States. South Carolina did that on December 20, 1860. Other Southern states soon followed.

They united to form a new country. It was called the Confederate States of America, or the **Confederacy** (kun-FEH-duh-ruh-see).

The Confederacy created a great **crisis**. A crisis is a dangerous situation. Lincoln said he would keep the **Union** (the whole country) together.

Confederate guns opened fire on Fort Sumter on April 14, 1861. The Civil War had started. The fort surrendered after more than a day of battle.

▲ Abraham Lincoln

▲ An 1860 newspaper announced the secession of South Carolina.

▲ Soldiers used cannons to destroy Fort Sumter.

▲ Dates indicate when each state seceded.

INTRODUCTION

Strengths and Weaknesses

In the Civil War, each side had strengths and weaknesses. The North had many more people than the South. It had more men who could become soldiers. It also had more factories, farms, and natural resources. This meant it could make more weapons, uniforms, and other things needed for war. It could grow more food to feed its armies. The North had more railroads, too. That meant it could ship soldiers and supplies more easily.

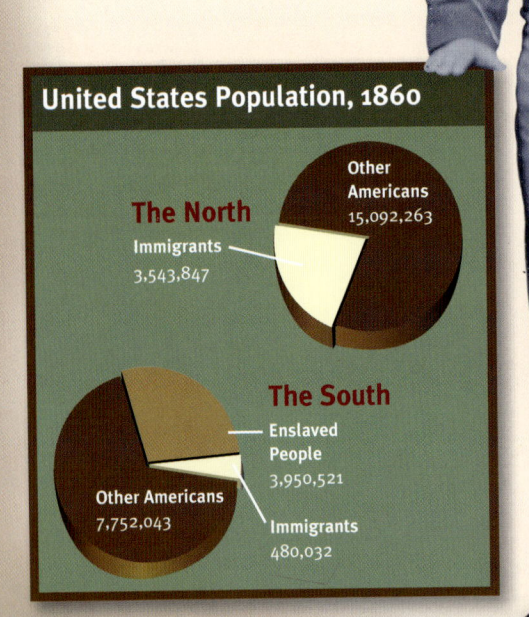

▲ a Confederate soldier

◀ a Union soldier

United States Population, 1860

The North
- Immigrants 3,543,847
- Other Americans 15,092,263

The South
- Enslaved People 3,950,521
- Immigrants 480,032
- Other Americans 7,752,043

INTRODUCTION

But the South had strengths, too. It had much better generals. This fact was not clear at the beginning of the war. But as the war went on, the South's generals were much more successful.

Southern soldiers also were highly **motivated** (MOH-tih-vay-ted). They had a very strong reason for fighting the war. Slavery was an important part of the way of life in the South. Southern soldiers were fighting for their way of life.

The South also was defending its own land. Southern soldiers were fighting on land they knew well. Northern armies had to invade the South. They had to fight on land they didn't know. They had to bring supplies from far away.

1 SOLVE THIS

In the election of 1860, the Democratic Party split into two parts. Use the information in the chart to estimate how many votes the two Democratic candidates together got in the election. (Hint: Round the numbers to the hundred thousands place.)

MATH ✓ POINT

What steps did you follow to get your answers?

| Presidential Election, 1860 |||
Candidate	Political Party	Popular Vote
Abraham Lincoln	Republican	1,865,908
Stephen A. Douglas	Northern Democrat	1,380,202
John Breckenridge	Southern Democrat	848,019
John Bell	Constitutional Union	590,901

CHAPTER 1

Background to Battle

The Union army and the Confederate army had their first battle in July 1861. It took place near Washington, D.C., at a creek called Bull Run. Hundreds of people rode out with the Union army to watch. Many brought picnics along. They were going to watch the battle. Instead they found themselves running for their lives along with the Union soldiers. The Battle of Bull Run showed that the Union army was not ready for war.

Picnickers in Washington, D.C. rode out to watch the battle. They had to flee when the Union army arrived. ▼

PRIMARY SOURCE

On April 9, 1862, President Lincoln sent the following message to General McClellan:

My dear Sir;
Your [message complaining that you do not have enough soldiers and supplies] . . . pain[s] me very much . . . I think it is the [right] time for you to strike a blow. By delay the enemy will . . . gain upon you. . . . And once more let me tell you, it is [important] that you strike a blow . . .

Yours very truly,
Lincoln

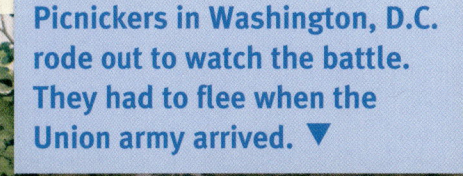

▲ the Battle of Bull Run

▲ General George McClellan

After Bull Run, Lincoln wanted a strong leader. He appointed General George McClellan to command the Union army.

At first, McClellan seemed to be an excellent choice to lead the Union army. He inspired his soldiers. He was also good at training and supplying the army. But Lincoln soon noticed something else about McClellan that was not good. McClellan was a very cautious general. He did not attack until he was absolutely sure of success. He did not take risks. Lincoln wanted action. McClellan said that the army was not ready.

CHAPTER 1

Robert E. Lee

General Robert E. Lee led the Confederate armies. He was a very different kind of leader than McClellan.

Robert E. Lee grew up in a military family in Virginia. His father, General "Light Horse" Harry Lee, had been a hero of the American Revolution. Robert E. Lee served in the United States Army most of his career. In 1861, President Lincoln asked Lee to become commander of the Union army. Lee was faced with a hard choice. He was opposed to slavery and secession, but he refused the offer. Lee told the president that his first loyalty was to Virginia. When Virginia left the Union, Lee resigned from the Union army.

PRIMARY SOURCE

There are few, I believe, in this . . . age, who will not agree that slavery. . . is a moral and political evil.

—Robert E. Lee

▲ Robert E. Lee

BACKGROUND TO BATTLE

Lee joined the Confederate army. In 1862, Confederate President Jefferson Davis appointed Lee to command the Army of Northern Virginia. Lee was also made commander of all the armies of the Confederacy.

Like McClellan, Lee inspired great loyalty in his men. But the way that they fought was very different. Lee took risks. He was daring. He often fought battles in which his soldiers were outnumbered. He used surprise and speed in battle to make up for having fewer soldiers.

▲ Jefferson Davis

It's a Fact

Arlington National Cemetery is located in Arlington, Virginia. It is where American war heroes, servicemen, and servicewomen are buried. The grounds of the cemetery were the home of Robert E. Lee. During the Civil War, the Union army took away Lee's land and house.

▲ Arlington National Cemetery

CHAPTER 1

Rising and Falling Fortunes

Both sides thought the war would end quickly. Both sides expected to win. There were few major battles in 1861. Neither army was ready to fight battle after battle. In the spring of 1862, the Union army won some important battles. General Ulysses S. Grant won important victories in Kentucky and Tennessee. He captured two Confederate forts. Then, in April 1862, Grant won the Battle of Shiloh (SHY-loh) in Tennessee.

▼ **General Ulysses S. Grant**

▼ **the Battle of Shiloh**

BACKGROUND TO BATTLE

▲ Battle of Shiloh

The Battle of Shiloh shocked both sides. No battle in American history had ever cost so many lives. Thousands of soldiers died. Thousands more were wounded. The fighting lasted just two days, but they were long and bloody days.

Grant's win in Tennessee cheered people in the North. But people in the South were badly frightened. They worried that the Union army would soon beat them and win the war.

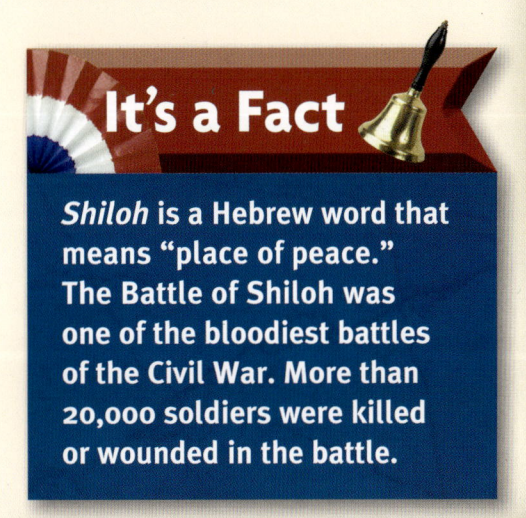

It's a Fact

Shiloh is a Hebrew word that means "place of peace." The Battle of Shiloh was one of the bloodiest battles of the Civil War. More than 20,000 soldiers were killed or wounded in the battle.

Robert E. Lee Strikes Back

In the summer of 1862, Robert E. Lee had the Army of Northern Virginia ready for battle. He quickly moved against the slow-moving McClellan. General Thomas "Stonewall" Jackson helped Lee. Jackson had already won several battles against McClellan. The two armies fought a weeklong battle in Virginia. It was called the Seven Days' Battle. Lee beat McClellan badly. McClellan thought that Lee had more men, so he was slow to attack. But this was not true. McClellan had more than twice the number of soldiers that Lee did. Lee's fast moves were successful. The Confederate army was now able to move close to Washington, D.C. This put the Union capital in

▼ Great Britain needed Southern cotton for its textile industry.

✔ POINT Visualize

Imagine you are Robert E. Lee or George McClellan. How does each man picture the Seven Days' Battle?

danger. Lincoln was angry with McClellan. He thought McClellan should have moved faster and attacked.

Diplomacy

The Civil War was more than a military war. It was also a diplomatic war. **Diplomacy** (dih-PLOH-muh-see) is the way countries get along with each other. The Confederacy hoped to get help from Great Britain and France. These two countries needed the cotton grown in the South. They used it for their **textile**, or clothing, industry. Both countries wanted to help the Confederacy. But first they needed to be sure the South had a good chance of beating the North.

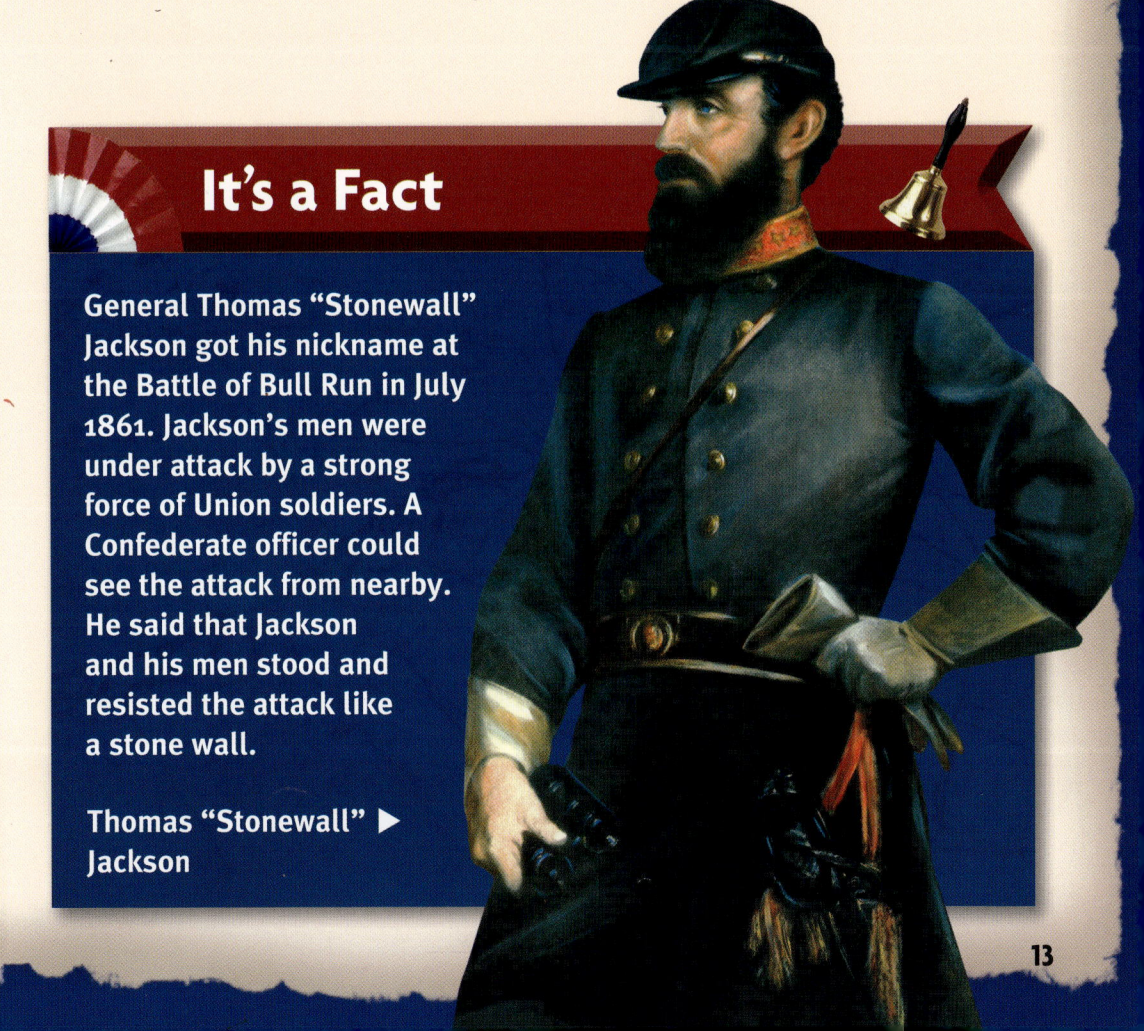

It's a Fact

General Thomas "Stonewall" Jackson got his nickname at the Battle of Bull Run in July 1861. Jackson's men were under attack by a strong force of Union soldiers. A Confederate officer could see the attack from nearby. He said that Jackson and his men stood and resisted the attack like a stone wall.

Thomas "Stonewall" ▶ Jackson

CHAPTER 2

The Bloodiest Day in American History

In September 1862, Lee decided to invade the North. He had several reasons for his decision. Lee had fought McClellan's army all summer. He thought he knew how to defeat McClellan. He saw that Confederate victories were causing the Northerners to lose hope. Lee hoped for a big victory in the North. The Northerners might then urge Lincoln to make peace.

Most of the fighting had taken place in Virginia. This was hard on Virginia farmers.

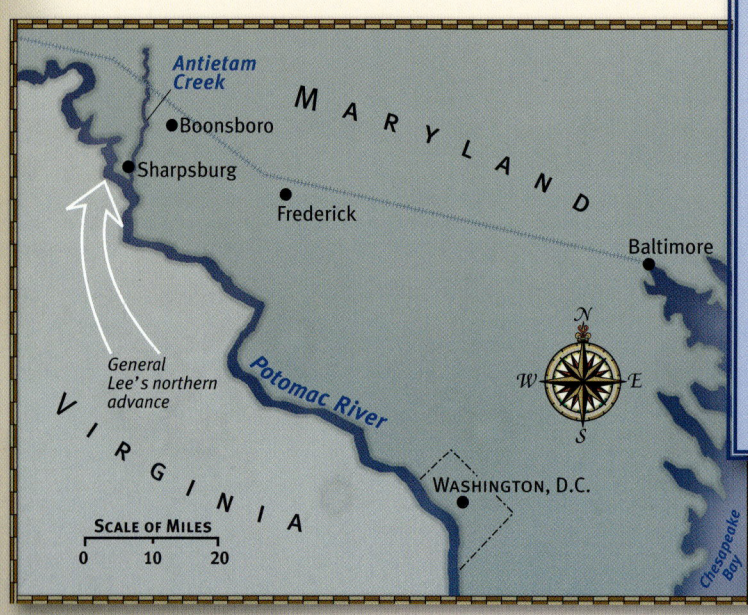

SOLVE THIS — 2

About how many miles separate Sharpsburg, Maryland, and Washington, D.C.?
a. 20   b. 45
c. 70   d. 125

MATH ✓ POINT

What steps did you follow to get your answer?

▲ Confederate cavalry crossing the Potomac River on June 11, 1863

Their farm fields had been turned into battlefields. September was harvest time. Taking the war to the North would protect Southern farms. Also, Lee's army was poorly fed and clothed. But Lee thought the soldiers could **plunder**, or steal, food from Northern farms.

Lee's army crossed the Potomac River. They invaded Maryland. People in Maryland were shocked at how Lee's army looked. Many soldiers were barefoot. Their uniforms were little more than rags. They were hungry and dirty.

The Army of Northern Virginia did not look like much, but its soldiers could fight. And they had a great leader in Robert E. Lee.

EYEWITNESS ACCOUNT

A person living in Maryland told a reporter from a Baltimore newspaper that he smelled Lee's army long before he saw them:

"*I have never seen a mess of such filthy strong-smelling men . . . They were the roughest set of [men] I ever saw, their . . . hair and clothing matted with dirt and filth.*"

CHAPTER 2

▲ Lee's lost order probably looked like this.

The Lost Orders

Battles are sometimes won or lost by a chance happening. On September 9, 1862, Lee gave orders to his commanders. Lee knew that he was badly outnumbered by McClellan. But he also knew how cautious McClellan was. Lee was daring. He split his army in two. He would attack McClellan from two different directions. The danger was that each part of the army would be even more heavily outnumbered. Lee counted on McClellan to move cautiously despite the split forces.

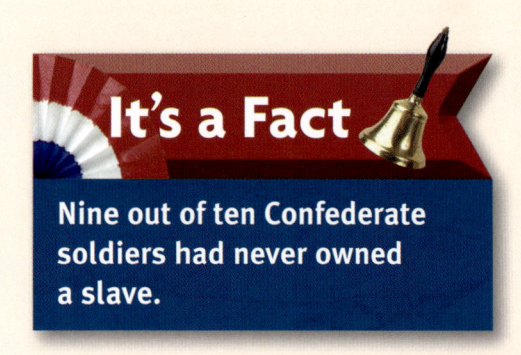

It's a Fact

Nine out of ten Confederate soldiers had never owned a slave.

THE BLOODIEST DAY IN AMERICAN HISTORY

On September 12, the two armies were moving toward each other. Corporal Barton Mitchell of the Union army was tired. When the army stopped to rest, Corporal Mitchell threw himself under a tree. Much to his surprise, he saw a paper wrapped around three cigars. When he looked more closely, Corporal Mitchell could not believe his eyes. The paper was Lee's orders to his generals. Mitchell brought the orders to headquarters. McClellan and his generals thought they had found the key to victory. Chance had worked in their favor.

They Made a Difference

Oliver Wendell Holmes, Jr. was an officer in the Union army. He was badly wounded three times. The last time was at Antietam where no one thought he would survive. He survived and lived to be 94. At the age of 61, Holmes was appointed to the U.S. Supreme Court. He was one of the most important justices ever to serve on the Court.

▲ Oliver Wendell Holmes, Jr.

CHAPTER 2

The Battle of Antietam

On September 17, 1862, the battle took place at last. The two armies met at Antietam Creek. It was near the town of Sharpsburg, Maryland. Different units of each army fought each other across a wide area. They fought a series of skirmishes. One of the most famous of these took place in a 30-acre (12-hectare) cornfield. The field was full of Confederate troops. Union forces attacked. The Confederates returned fire. The battle went on for an hour.

◀ Rufus Dawes

Rufus Dawes was a Union soldier in the battle. He wrote that before the battle, the corn stood taller than the soldiers.

THEY MADE A DIFFERENCE

There were no army nurses in the Civil War. Both armies used volunteers. Many of the volunteers were women. Clara Barton was with McClellan's army at the Battle of Antietam. She worked on the battlefield as the fighting raged. Barton later wrote about what happened as she was giving a wounded soldier a drink:

I bent down to give him a drink. I raised him with my right arm. Then I felt something shake the loose sleeve of my dress. At the same time, the poor fellow sprang from my arms and died. I realized a bullet had passed through my sleeve and hit him. There was no more to be done for him and I left him to rest.

THE BLOODIEST DAY IN AMERICAN HISTORY

"The men were loading and firing with . . . fury," Dawes recalled. "Men . . . were knocked out of the ranks by dozens. But we jumped over the fence, and pushed on, loading, firing, and shouting as we advanced. There was . . . great . . . excitement, eagerness to go forward, and a reckless disregard of life, of everything but victory."

At the end of the battle, the corn had been cut clean to the ground. There was not a stalk left. It was a bare field. This battle became known as "The Cornfield."

It's a Fact

The Battle of Antietam is also known as the Battle of Sharpsburg. Why does the battle have two names? The Union army named battles after nearby waterways. So they called the battle "Antietam" after Antietam Creek, which runs through the battlefield. The Confederacy named battles after nearby towns. The nearest town to the battle was Sharpsburg.

▼ Fierce fighting took place around the Roulette Farm during the Battle of Antietam.

Bloody Lane and Burnside's Bridge

Another part of the battle took place along a half-mile (.8-km) -long farm road. Wagon ruts in the ground were several feet (about one meter) deep. The ruts made a good place for Confederate soldiers to stop and fight. Wave after wave of Union troops attacked the Southerners along the road. The outnumbered Southern soldiers kept firing. After four hours, the Union troops were able to drive the Southerners off the road. But hundreds of Union and Confederate troops lay dead. The soldiers named the road "Bloody Lane."

▲ Burnside's Bridge as it looked during the Civil War and as it is today.

▲ The soldiers called this road "Bloody Lane."

THE BLOODIEST DAY IN AMERICAN HISTORY

At the same time, a battle was taking place at a small bridge across Antietam Creek. A group of about 600 Confederate soldiers held off a much larger force commanded by General Ambrose Burnside. Antietam Creek was only about 30 yards (about 27 meters) wide and not too deep. Union soldiers could have easily crossed at other places, but Burnside wanted to claim that bridge. He wanted to drive the Confederates off the bridge. The brave Confederates held out for almost four hours.

The Union won the fight at Burnside's Bridge. But the delay allowed Lee to attack Burnside with soldiers pulled from a different part of the battle. Burnside was trying to take control of the only road out of Sharpsburg. Because of the delay at what became known as Burnside's Bridge, Lee was able to keep control of the road. A day later, control of the road saved his army.

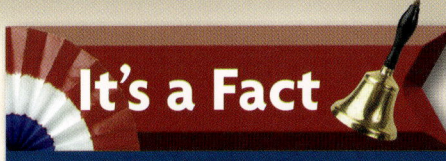

It's a Fact

The Battle of Antietam has not been forgotten. Every year a ceremony is held to remember the day. A candle is lit for each of the more than 23,000 people killed or wounded on both sides.

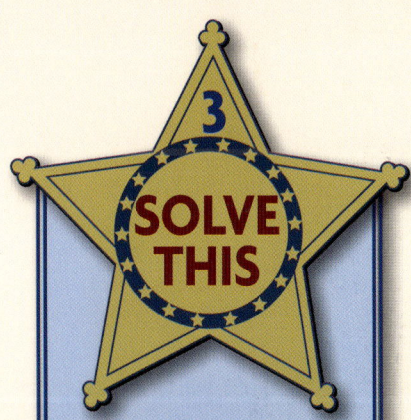

3 SOLVE THIS

Volunteers make the candles used in the ceremony. Each volunteer can work for 30 hours. If each volunteer can make four candles in an hour, how many volunteers are needed?

MATH ✓ POINT

What steps did you follow to get your answer?

CHAPTER 2

The Killing Fields

The Battle of Antietam ended at nightfall. Only then could both sides begin to count their losses. The final count took several days. Both McClellan and Lee realized that something terrible had taken place along the banks of Antietam Creek. There were more than 23,000 **casualties** at the Battle of Antietam. A casualty is a dead or wounded soldier. The chart shows the losses for each side.

On the morning of September 18, McClellan received **reinforcements** (ree-in-FORS-ments), or new troops. The Union army now far outnumbered the soldiers that Lee could put in the field. But McClellan was still too cautious. He knew that Lee had split his army. Yet McClellan still believed that the Southerners had more soldiers than he did. So he did not attack. Lee made use of McClellan's caution. He moved his army back across the Potomac River.

4 SOLVE THIS

How many more soldiers did the Union army have than the Confederate army? How many soldiers were killed altogether at the Battle of Antietam?

MATH ✓ POINT
What steps did you follow to get your answer?

Battle of Antietam Casualties

Army	Number of Soldiers in Battle	Killed	Wounded
Union	87,000	2,108	9,549
Confederate	45,000	1,546	9,024

THE BLOODIEST DAY IN AMERICAN HISTORY

Who won the Battle of Antietam? In military terms the battle was a **draw**, or a tie. Both sides lost about the same number of soldiers. But it was easier for the Union army to replace the lost soldiers. With Lee's **retreat**, McClellan proclaimed a great victory. Newspapers in the North celebrated the victory. Only President Lincoln was not happy with the outcome.

▼ The Union and Confederate armies lost thousands of men at the Battle of Antietam.

CHAPTER 3

A Different World

President Lincoln believed that McClellan could have finished off Lee's army on September 18. That might have ended the war. Instead, McClellan let Lee get away. Lincoln was angry. He wanted the war to stop. Then he had an idea.

▲ President Abraham Lincoln reading the Emancipation Proclamation

Lincoln saw an opportunity after the Battle of Antietam. The press was calling it a great Union victory. Lincoln decided to issue an important document. It was the Emancipation Proclamation. In it, Lincoln freed all the slaves in the Confederacy. This was a powerful law. Finally, slavery had ended.

But few slaves were freed right away. That was because the Union army did not control much of the South. But the Emancipation Proclamation expanded the goals of the Civil War. Now the war was not just being fought to preserve the Union. It was also being fought to end slavery.

✓ Point Reread

Reread pages 24–25. What made Lincoln decide to issue the Emancipation Proclamation?

EYEWITNESS ACCOUNT

Frederick Douglass was the most famous African American in the United States during the Civil War. Douglass had escaped from slavery. He was a leader in the fight against slavery. The Emancipation Proclamation took effect on January 1, 1863. Douglass wrote this about that day:

"The first of January, 1863, was a special day in the progress of American liberty and civilization. It was the turning point in the conflict between freedom and slavery. A death blow has been given to the slaveholding rebellion. We shout for joy that we live [to see this great day]."

Effects of the Emancipation Proclamation

The Emancipation Proclamation changed the rules. African Americans had not been allowed to join the Union army. Now they could, and they fought with pride and honor. The Confederacy did not allow slaves to join its army. The North now had more men joining its army and ready to fight.

The Emancipation Proclamation had another effect. It encouraged slaves in the South to run away. The escaping African Americans did not have to reach Northern states. They only had to get as far as Union army lines to find freedom.

Historical Perspective

The Emancipation Proclamation changed the position of the United States on slavery. At the Constitutional Convention, the Founding Fathers could not agree on slavery and freedom. It took the Civil War to finally solve that conflict. In 1865, President Lincoln urged the Congress to pass the 13th Amendment to the U.S. Constitution. It ended slavery everywhere in the United States.

▲ More than 180,000 African American soldiers served bravely in the war. About 37,000 of them died.

A DIFFERENT WORLD

▲ By the end of the war, nearly one million enslaved African Americans had escaped. That was about one-quarter of all the slaves in the South.

PRIMARY SOURCE

The *New York Tribune* newspaper greeted the news of the Emancipation Proclamation with this editorial written by its editor, Horace Greeley:
GOD BLESS ABRAHAM LINCOLN!
. . . *It is the beginning of the end of the rebellion; the beginning of the new life of the nation.*

The Emancipation Proclamation also ended any chance that France and Great Britain would help the Confederacy. Both countries were against slavery. They decided not to help the South.

The Emancipation Proclamation helped Lincoln win more support in the North. Many people wanted Lincoln to take a stronger stand against slavery. The Emancipation Proclamation helped bring the people in the North together. Most Northerners were now committed to winning the war.

The reaction in the South was quite different. People were furious. A Richmond, Virginia, newspaper wrote that the Emancipation Proclamation was "a bid for the slaves to rise in rebellion." To some, it was the end of a way of life.

A Long War

The Civil War raged on for almost three years after the Battle of Antietam. In November 1862, Lincoln, tired of McClellan's excuses, fired the general. His replacements did not do much better. The North had several chances to end the war, but its generals did not act fast enough. The fast-moving and daring Lee could not be stopped. Many people wondered how long the war would last. A war that most people had thought would last no more than a year was still going with no end in sight.

In July 1863, Lee once more invaded the North. Union forces defeated him at the Battle of Gettysburg. But once again, Union forces did not follow up their victory. Lee managed to withdraw to safety. Could anyone ever stop Lee?

In 1864, Lincoln appointed General Ulysses S. Grant commander of the Union army. Grant was not like earlier commanders. He knew that he had to stop Lee. He had to make daring moves. He chased Lee all over Virginia. Lee was skillful enough to make the war last a year longer. But in April 1865, Lee surrendered. The war was finally over.

It's a Fact

Paper money first came into use in the United States during the Civil War. The Confederacy was in bad financial condition. It could not get loans to finance the war effort. By 1864, the paper money issued by the Confederacy reached $1 billion. There was so much confederate paper money printed it became almost worthless. There was not enough gold in the treasury to support all the paper currency.

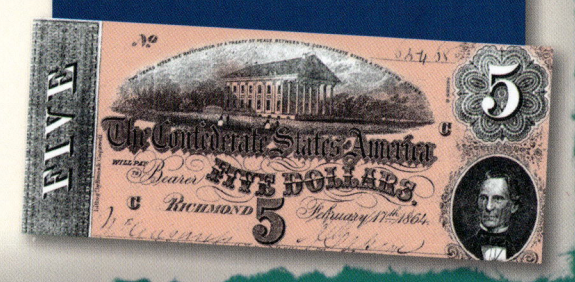

Conclusion

The Battle of Antietam helped decide the outcome of the war. If Lee had won the battle, many things might have changed. It is likely that Great Britain and France would have sided with the Confederacy. Maybe people in the North, tired of the fighting, would have forced Lincoln to make peace. The country would have remained divided. Slavery would have continued, and the history of the United States and the history of the world would have been very different.

Cause	Effect
Lincoln is elected president.	Southern states secede.
The Confederacy attacks Fort Sumter.	The Civil War starts.
McClellan does not attack Lee's army on September 18, 1862.	Lee's army escapes.
Battle of Antietam is seen as a victory for Union forces.	Lincoln issues the Emancipation Proclamation.
Emancipation Proclamation	Ending slavery becomes a goal for the North.
Emancipation Proclamation	African Americans are allowed to join Union army.
Emancipation Proclamation	Great Britain and France are convinced to support the North.

SOLVE THIS

Answers

1. Page 5
The two Democratic candidates together got 2,200,000 votes (rounded).
Stephen A. Douglas (Northern Democrat) = 1,400,000
John Breckenridge (Southern Democrat) = 800,000
 1,400,000 + 800,000 = 2,200,000 total Democratic votes

2. Page 14
c. 70

3. Page 21
Each volunteer can make about 120 candles.
4 candles/hour x 30 hours = 120 candles per volunteer
About 192 volunteers are needed.
23,000 candles needed/120 candles per volunteer = about 192 volunteers

4. Page 22
The Union had 42,000 more soldiers than the Confederacy.
87,000 – 45,000 = 42,000
There were 3,654 soldiers killed at the Battle of Antietam.
2,108 + 1,546 = 3,654

Glossary

casualty — (KA-zhul-tee) a dead or wounded soldier (page 22)

Confederacy — (kun-FEH-duh-ruh-see) the eleven Southern states that declared themselves separate from the United States in 1860 and 1861 (page 2)

crisis — (KRY-sis) a difficult or dangerous situation (page 2)

diplomacy — (dih-PLOH-muh-see) the ways countries get along with each other (page 13)

draw — (DRAW) a tie (page 23)

motivate — (MOH-tih-vate) to move someone to action (page 5)

plunder — (PLUN-der) to steal (page 15)

reinforcements — (ree-in-FORS-ments) additional soldiers (page 22)

retreat — (rih-TREET) to move back (page 23)

secede — (sih-SEED) to withdraw from a group or organization (page 2)

territory — (TAIR-ih-tor-ee) a settled area belonging to the United States that is not yet a state (page 2)

textile — (TEK-stile) related to the making of cloth (page 13)

Union — (YOON-yun) the states that stayed loyal to the federal government during the Civil War (page 2)

Index

Army of Northern Virginia, 9, 12, 15
Battle of Antietam, 18–19, 21–23, 25, 28–29
Battle of Bull Run, 6–7
Battle of Gettysburg, 28
Battle of Shiloh, 10–11
"Bloody Lane," 20
Burnside, General Ambrose, 21
Burnside's Bridge, 20–21
casualty, 22
Confederacy, 2, 6, 8–10, 12–15, 19–23, 25–29
crisis, 2
Davis, Jefferson, 9
diplomacy, 13
draw, 23
Emancipation Proclamation, 25–27
Fort Sumter, 2
France, 13, 27, 29
Grant, General Ulysses S., 10–11, 28
Great Britain, 13, 27, 29
Jackson, General Thomas "Stonewall," 12

Lee, General Robert E., 8–9, 12, 14–17, 21–24, 28–29
Lincoln, Abraham, 2, 5–8, 13–14, 23–29
Maryland, 15, 18
McClellan, General George, 6–9, 12–14, 16–18, 22–24, 28–29
Mitchell, Corporal Barton, 17
motivate, 5
plunder, 15
reinforcements, 22
retreat, 23
secede, 2
Seven Days' Battle, 12
slavery, 2, 5, 8, 25–27, 29
South Carolina, 2
territory, 2
textile, 13
Union, 2, 6–13, 17–23, 25–26, 28–29
Virginia, 8–9, 12, 14–15, 27–28
Washington, D.C., 6, 12

Taking Care of Earth

Copyright © by Harcourt, Inc.

All rights reserved. No part of this publication may be reproduced or transmitted in any form or by any means, electronic or mechanical, including photocopy, recording, or any information storage and retrieval system, without permission in writing from the publisher.

Requests for permission to make copies of any part of the work should be addressed to School Permissions and Copyrights, Harcourt, Inc., 6277 Sea Harbor Drive, Orlando, Florida 32887-6777. Fax: 407-345-2418.

HARCOURT and the Harcourt Logo are trademarks of Harcourt, Inc., registered in the United States of America and/or other jurisdictions.

Printed in Mexico

ISBN-13: 978-0-15-362248-9
ISBN-10: 0-15-362248-2

2 3 4 5 6 7 8 9 10   050   16 15 14 13 12 11 10 09 08

Harcourt
SCHOOL PUBLISHERS

Visit *The Learning Site!*
www.harcourtschool.com

What Are Natural Resources?

You walk on it. You run on it. Your school is built on it. Earth is your home! Have you ever thought about all of the things that Earth provides?

Earth provides air for you to breathe, water for you to drink, and the soil needed to grow the food you eat. Air, water, and soil are three natural resources essential for your life. Natural resources are materials on Earth that are necessary or useful to people.

What are some other ways you use natural resources? Your clothes are made from natural resources. So are the books you read and the chairs you sit in. Schools, homes, bridges, walls, sidewalks, and roads are all made with natural resources.

Soil is a natural resource. Soil is important for growing plants, including many of the foods you eat each day!

This building is made of stone. Rocks are an important natural resource.

Light in your home and school is produced from natural resources. So is the energy to heat or cool them. The gasoline used to power buses and cars comes from a natural resource, too. You could not cook your dinner, wash your clothes, or listen to music without natural resources!

MAIN IDEA AND DETAILS List three natural resources you have used today.

Renewable and Nonrenewable Resources

Some of the resources you use every day are renewable. A **renewable resource** is a resource that can be replaced or is reusable. A resource that is reusable can be used over and over again.

One example of a renewable resource is water. The water you use each day is part of the water cycle. The water cycle moves water between Earth and the atmosphere. It makes water usable again and again. Air is another renewable resource. Renewable resources such as water and air can be used over and over only if people use them carefully.

Some natural resources you use each day are nonrenewable. A **nonrenewable resource** is a resource that cannot be replaced in your lifetime. Many energy sources are nonrenewable. Coal and oil are two sources of energy that take a very long time to form. Other nonrenewable resources include minerals and rocks.

Water and air are resources that are essential to life.

Rich soil has lots of nutrients that plants can use and is good for growing crops.

Soil and some plants are essentially nonrenewable resources. Soil forms when weathered rock mixes with organic matter, water, and air. Rich soil has minerals and other nutrients needed for plants. It takes thousands of years to form a few inches of soil. Plants grown on farms are renewable resources. Some plants, such as those in old-growth forests, take hundreds of years to grow. Once they are cut down, it will take a very long time to replace them.

MAIN IDEA AND DETAILS Name one renewable resource and one nonrenewable resource.

Air Pollution

People add materials to Earth's air as they use it. For example, cars, buses, trains, airplanes, and factories all add gases and chemicals to the air. These gases and chemicals can cause serious problems.

You may have seen pictures of a yellow or brown haze over a city. This haze is called *smog*. Smog is a mixture of smoke, chemicals, and water vapor. Smog is an example of air pollution. **Pollution** is a waste product that harms living things and damages an ecosystem. Air pollution occurs when harmful substances get into air. Air pollution is just one kind of pollution. Water and land can be polluted, too.

Fast Fact

The United States government established the Environmental Protection Agency (EPA) in 1970. The EPA works to help control pollution from cars and sets standards for a healthy environment.

Smog is often produced where there are a large number of vehicles or factories.

Cars are a big source of pollution. Although today's cars produce less pollution than older cars, there are more cars on the roads.

Most air pollution is caused by the burning of fuels. Coal, oil, gasoline, and diesel fuel are examples of fuels that release harmful substances into the air when they are burned. You see air pollution caused by diesel fuel when you see black smoke coming from the back of a bus.

Air pollution can cause big problems in people's health. These health problems include eye irritations and breathing problems. The United States has passed laws to help control air pollution. These laws place restrictions on the amounts and types of chemicals vehicles and factories can release.

MAIN IDEA AND DETAILS What are the major causes of air pollution?

Water Pollution

Pollution in the air can lead to acid rain. Vehicles and energy stations release chemicals into the air that can mix with water in the air to form acids. These acids fall to the ground as acid rain. Acid rain falls on rivers, lakes, and land. It can kill fish when it falls in lakes. It can damage trees and kill plants when it falls on land. Acid rain can even damage buildings. The acids in the water react with the building stone and wear it away.

Acid rain is produced when harmful substances from the air enter the water cycle. Harmful substances enter the water cycle in other ways, as well. Factories and mines may dump harmful wastes into rivers and lakes. These wastes also may get into groundwater. Fertilizers and pesticides used by farmers or home gardeners wash into water supplies, too.

Fast Fact

Algae blooms occur when algae multiply suddenly and rapidly. They may turn water neon blue or green and cause a bad smell. When the algae die, decomposers may deplete all the oxygen in the water, killing fish.

Acid rain causes the erosion of buildings and other structures.

Another source of water pollution is *sewage.* Sewage is human waste that is generally flushed away to a sewage treatment facility. However, sewage can get into water supplies that people use for drinking, cooking, or bathing. This can make people sick.

Laws to control water pollution require people to clean water before the water goes back into the water cycle.

Focus Skill

MAIN IDEA AND DETAILS What causes acid rain to form?

Water pollution could kill many plants and animals in this healthy ecosystem.

Land Pollution

In some places, land is polluted by enormous amounts of trash. Many materials in garbage dumps or landfills take a very long time to break down. This is especially true of materials, such as plastics, made by humans. Sometimes garbage contains harmful chemicals that soak into the ground and get into water supplies.

Industrial wastes can also harm land. These poisonous wastes are sometimes buried in large containers in the ground. The containers may leak or break, allowing poison to pollute the ground.

Land also can be misused. For example, land is misused when good farming practices are not used. Good farming practices include planting cover crops to protect unused land. Cover crops are not for harvesting. They are planted in empty fields. The plants' roots hold soil in place. Without cover crops or other protection, wind and water may carry away soil. Soil is a valuable natural resource that takes thousands of years to replace.

As Earth's population grows, more trash is produced.

The dust clouds that formed in the 1930s in the Great Plains were so large that they buried fences, houses, and buildings when they settled. This was known as the Dust Bowl.

Communities are working to stop land pollution and misuse. Many farmers protect their fields. Many people and companies dispose of wastes in ways that do not pollute land. The federal and state governments spend money to clean up poisons that have polluted land.

Fast Fact

In the 1930s, farmers on the Great Plains dug up millions of acres of land to grow crops. During a long, dry period, many plants died, and the soil dried out. Winds blew around huge clouds of dust, because there were no plants to hold the soil in place.

MAIN IDEA AND DETAILS
Why is protecting unused land important?

Conserving Resources

There are many people and other living things on Earth. All need to use Earth's resources. Everyone can help protect Earth's resources by practicing conservation. **Conservation** is preserving and protecting natural resources. When you conserve something, you save it for future use.

One way to conserve resources is to *reduce* the resources used. You use less when you reduce. You can reduce the trash you produce by buying products with less packaging. You can take shorter showers to reduce your use of water. You can use appliances like air conditioners, lamps, and hair dryers less. You can walk to the store instead of driving. This saves energy and reduces the pollution caused by burning fuels.

Plastic food containers can be used over and over again.

You can also conserve resources by *reusing* and *recycling*. Reusing items means you use them again. For example, you can reuse a plastic container to hold pens and pencils. You can reuse gift-wrapping, donate clothing and toys you've outgrown to thrift shops, and buy used items.

Items that are recycled are changed into new items. Aluminum, glass, and paper can be treated so that they can be used to make new items. Recycling saves energy as well as resources. It takes less energy to make an item from recycled materials than it does to make it from raw resources. Recycling saves resources and reduces pollution.

> **Fast Fact**
>
> **Did you know that the numbers inside the recycling symbol on plastic containers are codes? The number tells the recycling plant what type of material the container is made from!**

Focus Skill **CAUSE AND EFFECT** How does recycling reduce pollution?

Today, many items can be recycled. Try to recycle whenever you can.

Ways to Conserve Soil and Water

Farmers have developed specific methods for conserving soil. Planting rows of trees or erecting fences between fields helps break the force of wind. Gentle winds do not carry as much soil away as strong winds. Crops can also be planted in rows around hills. This is called contour plowing. It prevents water from flowing quickly downhill and removing soil. Farmers also rotate crops. This means they change the plants they grow from year to year. Growing the same crops each year causes soil to lose important nutrients.

To create a windbreak, rows of trees are planted between fields of crops.

A leaky faucet wastes lots of water! A faucet dripping 20 times per minute wastes about 700 gallons a year.

Water is a renewable resource, but it is still precious. In the western United States, where it is drier, farmers conserve water by growing crops that do not need much water. They have also developed new ways of irrigating their crops. Communities and homeowners can conserve water by planting native plants that don't require much water. Individuals can use water responsibly, too. They can fix leaky faucets and use less water to wash dishes and cars.

MAIN IDEA AND DETAILS Explain one method farmers use to conserve soil.

Summary

You depend on many natural resources each day. Some of these resources are renewable, and others are nonrenewable. The pollution of air, water, and land can harm resources people and other living things need. You can help conserve resources by reducing, reusing, and recycling.

Glossary

conservation (kahn•ser•VAY•shuhn) The wise use of resources to make the supply last longer (12, 13, 14, 15)

nonrenewable resource (nahn•rih•NOO•uh•buhl REE•sawrs) A resource that, once used, cannot be replaced in a reasonable amount of time (4, 5, 15)

pollution (puh•LOO•shuhn) A waste product that harms living things and damages an ecosystem (6, 7, 8, 9, 10, 11, 12, 13, 15)

renewable resource (rih•NOO•uh•buhl REE•sawrs) A resource that can be replaced within a reasonable amount of time (4, 5, 15)

Powerful Oceans

Copyright © by Harcourt, Inc.

All rights reserved. No part of this publication may be reproduced or transmitted in any form or by any means, electronic or mechanical, including photocopy, recording, or any information storage and retrieval system, without permission in writing from the publisher.

Requests for permission to make copies of any part of the work should be addressed to School Permissions and Copyrights, Harcourt, Inc., 6277 Sea Harbor Drive, Orlando, Florida 32887-6777. Fax: 407-345-2418.

HARCOURT and the Harcourt Logo are trademarks of Harcourt, Inc., registered in the United States of America and/or other jurisdictions.

Printed in Mexico

ISBN-13: 978-0-15-362252-6
ISBN-10: 0-15-362252-0

2 3 4 5 6 7 8 9 10   050   16 15 14 13 12 11 10 09 08

Harcourt
SCHOOL PUBLISHERS

Visit *The Learning Site!*
www.harcourtschool.com

What Is Ocean Water Like?

About three-fourths of Earth's surface is covered by water. Most of it is contained in Earth's oceans and seas. Ocean water's most obvious characteristic is its saltiness. Oceans and seas are salty because of minerals dissolved in the water. Minerals dissolved from surrounding landforms are carried into the ocean by the water cycle. The main mineral dissolved in ocean water is halite—sodium chloride—or, table salt.

Salinity is the amount of salt in water. The salinity of ocean water doesn't change much from place to place. But some bodies of water are saltier than others. The Dead Sea is a landlocked sea in Israel. More water evaporates from it than flows into it, so it is 10 times saltier than the oceans.

From space it is easy to see that much of Earth's surface is covered by water.

Submersibles help humans explore the ocean depths. Scientists have found new species in the ocean depths.

Ocean water is not only salty, it's dark and cold. The deeper you go, the darker and colder it gets. The temperature of ocean waters depends on the water depth. Surface water is warmed by the sun and air. But most of the ocean is deep. Water absorbs and scatters light. The water gets darker and darker until there is no light at all.

Water pressure also changes with water depth. **Water pressure** is the downward push of water. It increases the deeper down you go in the ocean because more water is pushing down. Water pressure crushes most objects at great depths.

Fast Fact

To explore ocean depths, scientists use small submarines called submersibles. A submersible has very thick walls, which keep it from being crushed by water pressure.

MAIN IDEA AND DETAILS What are four characteristics of ocean waters?

What Is the Ocean Floor Like?

You have learned that land has different shapes. In some places there are valleys, and in others there are mountains. The ocean floor also has landforms. In some places it slopes gently, in other places it is flat. There are valleys, mountains, and even volcanoes.

A shallow area called the **continental shelf** extends into the ocean around the edges of the continents. Beyond the continental shelf is the **continental slope.** This area is steeper, deeper, and narrower than the continental shelf. The largest and flattest parts of the ocean floor are the **abyssal plains**. However, the abyssal plains are not completely flat. There are deep trenches and underwater mountains, too.

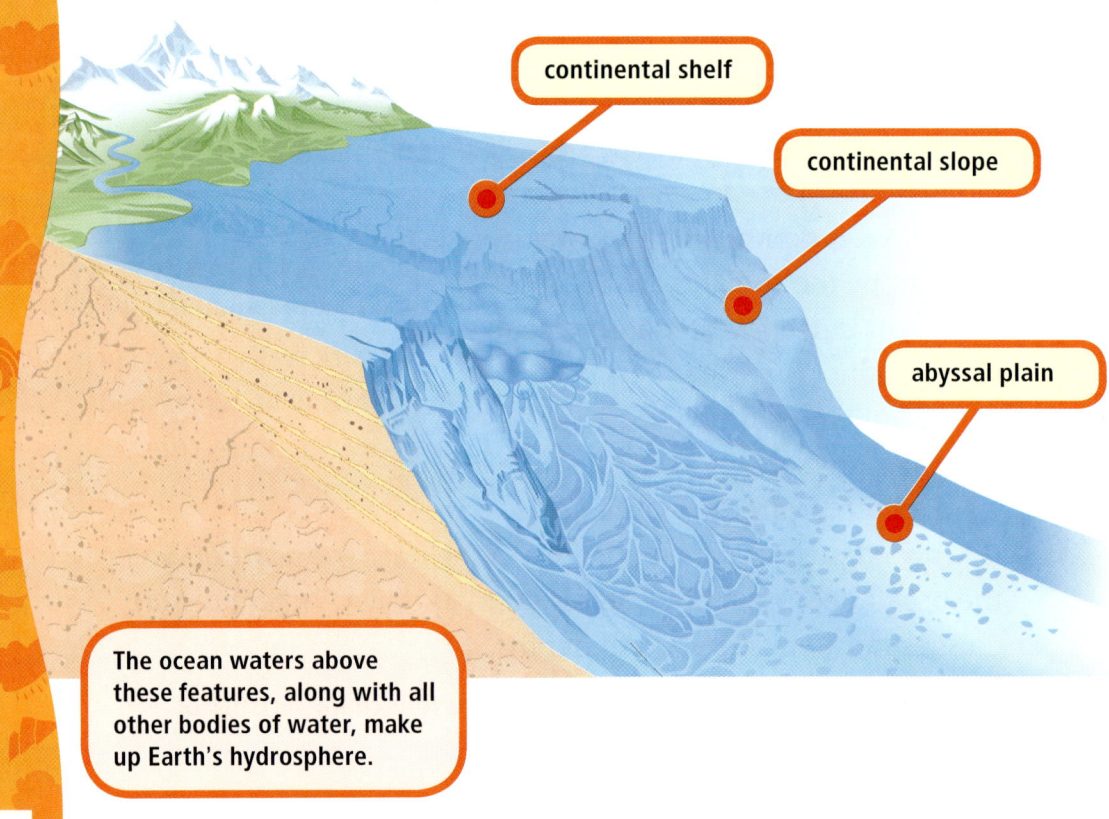

continental shelf

continental slope

abyssal plain

The ocean waters above these features, along with all other bodies of water, make up Earth's hydrosphere.

The ocean floor changes over time, just as land changes. Underwater volcanoes erupt. The tops of volcanoes extend above the ocean's surface in some places. Eruptions may form chains of islands. Islands that are formed in the ocean can change, too. Ocean waves wear away at rock. Islands may sink and eventually disappear beneath the water.

Focus Skill

MAIN IDEA AND DETAILS How is the continental shelf different from the continental slope?

The island of Surtsey is off the coast of Iceland. It formed from volcanic eruptions that occurred in the 1960s.

Ocean Waves

Ocean waters never stop moving. Most of the movement of water on the ocean's surface is due to waves. The waves may look as if they are moving across the ocean, but waves of water do not travel across the ocean. Waves only move up and down. A **wave** is an up-and-down movement of surface water.

Most waves are caused by wind. When wind blows over the surface of a body of water, it causes the surface of the water to move with it. Water moves more slowly than air, so it piles up, forming a ripple. The wind pushes on the ripple, making it grow. The ripple turns into a wave.

The energy carried by waves can change shorelines.

Energy, not water, is carried by a wave. That energy moves across the water, but the water itself turns in small circles and returns to about the same place it started. If you've ever watched a toy boat bobbing on the surface of the water, you've seen how waves pull the boat up, around, down, and back. The toy boat is returned to almost the same spot as it started.

As a wave approaches land, it begins to slow down. The bottom of the wave slows down more than the top, so the wave gets taller. The tall wave reaches a point where it collapses, or breaks, against the shore.

Fast Fact

The energy of an earthquake or volcano can produce gigantic waves called tsunamis. In 1958, a tsunami in Alaska reached a height of 524 meters (1,720 feet)!

COMPARE AND CONTRAST How is the motion of water in an ocean wave different from the motion of energy in an ocean wave?

The force of a breaking wave can be powerful. Over time, waves break rocks apart and smooth their surfaces.

Ocean Currents

Ocean waters are constantly pushed around the planet by currents. A **current** is a stream of water that flows like a river through the ocean. Some currents are on the ocean surface. Others are deep beneath the surface of the water. What causes surface currents? Energy from the sun heats the air around the equator. The air moves north toward the North Pole and south toward the South Pole. The moving air pushes ocean water along, too.

Surface currents carry water great distances. The Gulf Stream is a surface current in the Atlantic Ocean. It carries water from the Gulf of Mexico north along the eastern coast of the United States. The current then travels eastward and flows across the Atlantic Ocean to Europe.

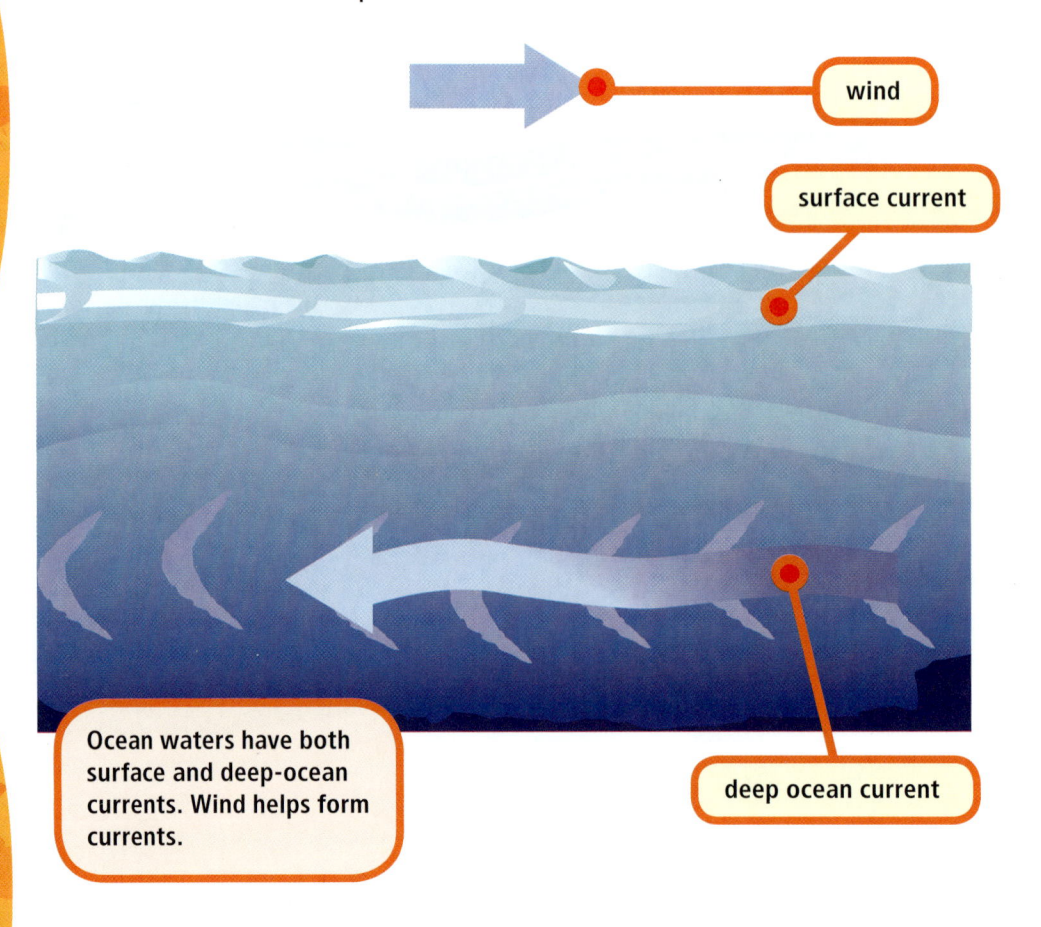

wind

surface current

Ocean waters have both surface and deep-ocean currents. Wind helps form currents.

deep ocean current

Deep water currents move far beneath the ocean surface. They are set into motion by changes in water temperature. For example, in some areas, winds blow warm surface water away from land. Cooler water moves up toward the surface near the coast as the warm water moves away. This creates a deep water current.

El Niño—a change in weather patterns over the Pacific Ocean—is caused by differences in water currents. Heavy rains from it can cause flooding.

Changes in wind patterns can alter these currents. If the wind changes direction and does not blow warm water away from the land, the warm water stays near the coast. Warm water off the coast affects weather patterns. There is more rain on the coasts near the warm water.

COMPARE AND CONTRAST How are surface currents different from deep water currents?

Ocean Tides

The level of the ocean water rises and falls each day. This repeated rise and fall of the water level is called the **tide**. Tides are a result of the pull of gravity of the sun and the moon on Earth's waters. Although the moon is much smaller than the sun, it is much closer to Earth. So the moon affects Earth's tides more.

The moon pulls on the whole planet. However, the water moves a lot more than the land. The pull of the moon combines with Earth's rotation to produce traveling bulges of water. Bulges of water form on each side of Earth.

One bulge of water forms on the side of Earth facing the moon. The other bulge is on the opposite side of Earth. The pull of the moon is slightly less on the opposite side, so the bulge of water is slightly smaller too. The bulges of water on either side of Earth are called high tides. Low water levels between high tides are called low tides. Most coastal areas have two high tides and two low tides every 24 hours.

COMPARE AND CONTRAST How is the sun's pull on the ocean different than the moon's pull?

At low tide, the water level of the ocean is lower. You see more land at the beach.

At high tide, the water level of the ocean is higher. You see less land at the beach.

11

At the Shore

The **shore** is the area where the ocean and land meet and interact. If you have visited different beaches, you know that each shore has unique features.

Shores are flat at some places. They may be covered with sand or small pebbles. Ocean currents can move sand, pebbles, and shells along the shore. Currents slow down and deposit materials picked up from the beach. New beaches may form, or an existing beach may acquire new sand.

There may be a steep cliff along a shore. The action of waves can erode the rock at the bottom of a cliff. Cliffs may eventually fall into the ocean.

Waves throw sand and pebbles against the shore. The water's motion and grinding of the sand and pebbles has eroded the cliff.

Pools of seawater called **tide pools** can be found along the shore, on rocky beaches. At high tide, these pools are under water. Some animals are free to move in or out of these pools. At low tide, the pools are trapped between rocks as the tide goes out. The animals are trapped, too, until the water rises again. Some plants and animals live their entire lives in tide pools.

An estuary is formed in places where rivers flow into oceans. An estuary has a mixture of fresh water and salt water. These areas are usually rich in animal and plant life.

MAIN IDEA AND DETAILS How can the movement of ocean currents affect the shape of a shore?

Tide pools are ideal habitats for a variety of animals and plants.

How Humans Affect the Shore

Ocean waves and currents change the shapes of shores. These are natural processes of erosion and deposition. Human activities can also change the shore. People in coastal communities may replace sand lost from beaches. They also may build structures to protect beaches from erosion. These structures block currents and change the natural processes of erosion.

A **jetty** is a structure made of rocks that sticks out into the ocean. It looks like a rock wall. A jetty protects the beach by trapping the sand and rocks that would be pulled away by ocean currents. But while one part of the beach is protected, the other is not. The beach below the jetty does not get the sand and rocks it would normally get.

MAIN IDEA AND DETAILS How do humans change the natural processes of erosion at beaches?

People build structures like this fence to protect beaches from erosion.

Jetties like this one can stop the erosion of sand from beaches.

Summary

Earth is covered by large bodies of salt water called the oceans. Ocean water is salty, and most of it is very deep, dark, and cold. Features of the ocean floor include valleys, mountains, and plains. The ocean is in constant motion. Ocean waters move as waves, currents, and tides. The shore is the area where land and water meet. The shore is constantly changed by the motion of waves, currents, and tides, and by human activities.

Glossary

abyssal plain (uh•BIS•uhl PLAYN) A large, flat area of the ocean floor (4)

continental shelf (kahnt•uhn•ENT•uhl SHELF) The shallow part of the ocean floor near the land (4, 5)

continental slope (kahnt•uhn•ENT•uhl SLOHP) The part of the ocean floor that slopes steeply (4, 5)

current (KUR•uhnt) A stream of water that flows like a river through the ocean (8, 9, 12, 13, 14, 15)

jetty (JET•ee) A wall-like structure that sticks out into the ocean to prevent sand from being carried away (14)

salinity (suh•LIN•uh•tee) The amount of salt in water (2)

shore (SHAWR) The area where the ocean and the land meet and interact (7, 12, 13, 14, 15)

tide (TYD) The rise and fall of the water level of the ocean (10, 11, 13, 15)

tide pool (TYD POOL) A temporary pool of ocean water that gets trapped between rocks when the tide goes out (13)

water pressure (WAWT•er PRESH•er) The downward push of water (3)

wave (WAYV) The up-and-down movement of surface water (5, 6, 7, 12, 14, 15)